Betty Aner 2010

Against All Odds:
Artist Dean Mitchell's Story

by

Betty R. James

FATHER & SON
PUBLISHING, INC.
4909 N. Monroe Street
Tallahassee, Florida 32303
http://www.fatherson.com
800-741-2712

Foreword

After reading this poignant story by my friend Betty James, I quietly sat in my favorite chair in the family room, closed my eyes, and reflected for a moment on the well-crafted words and paintings. Of course, this is my usual reaction when I read or view something moving, something powerful. My first thoughts were how pleased I was that Betty developed and wrote this story about a brave and talented young man who did not give up on his dreams. My thoughts turned back to my own personal and professional challenges and I quickly thought of a very famous quote that served as an anchor for my personal journey in life, by Richard M. DeVos: *"If I had to select one quality, one personal characteristic that I regard as being most highly correlated with success, whatever the field, I would pick the trait of persistence....*

For many of us, it is difficult to develop an insatiable desire to launch our own destiny, to achieve a goal and gain recognition. However, we must believe in ourselves. We must realize that sometimes in life, our victories don't come without adversity. We must always remember that the challenges and obstacles we face in life are not there to break us, but to create us. We must keep the faith and work hard to overcome them. We must persist for persistence is one of those positive, personal characteristics necessary for any successful venture.

There are dozens of youth who possess undeveloped talents similar to Dean Mitchell. This book should inspire youth who may be facing some of the same challenges as Dean Mitchell. Whether these challenges are associated with academics, personal talents, sports, or even public speaking. The reader will be encouraged not to give up and continue to persist, persist, and persist, until skills are mastered.

We have to learn to see ourselves as the driver of our own life. When we work hard on any worthwhile goal, our motivation will not always remain at the same level. Sometimes, we will feel motivated; sometimes we won't. But, it is not our motivation that will produce positive results—it is our action, our hard work. Persistence will ultimately provide its own motivation. Persistence equates to taking action, so keep working diligently.

For readers acquainted with the life and works of Dean Mitchell, this book becomes a unique treasure to be passed down through generations as a memento to overcoming obstacles and challenges while rising to national prominence. This is a story that will leave an indelible impression on the reader. However, I must post a warning; you will want to maintain several copies, as you will want every youth who may be faced with or who you perceive to be faced with challenges, whether you know them personally or not, to have a copy of, *Against All Odds: Artist Dean Mitchell's Story*.

Patricia Green-Powell, Ph.D.
Associate Professor of Educational Leadership
Florida A&M University
Tallahassee, Florida

Dedication

This book is a gift for my grandchildren,
Alexys, Brakayla, Gene-Reginald, and Brandon, Jr.

and

written to celebrate the gift of art
education for all children.

Table of Contents

Introduction

As a teacher, I have always enjoyed creating and writing stories, but this is the first published as a book. I was drawn to Dean Mitchell some years ago when I learned that this talented young artist was from my hometown of Quincy, Florida. Dean was raised by his grandmother who instilled in him a set of values that motivated him to achieve beyond the normal expectations of a small-town Southerner with many odds against him. The story of Dean Mitchell deserves to be told. His success stands as a lesson for achievement.

His art career began at age twelve when he purchased his first paint-by-number oil art set from a small store in Quincy. Today, he is famous for his immaculate watercolor and oil paintings found in art galleries throughout the United States.

I feel that Dean is a role model worthy of emulation by today's children. His artistic excellence is celebrated by people of every generation. Dean is a humble young man with something great to share with everyone. His passion for the simple things in life and the vignettes of real life he chronicles through his paintings relate to young and old alike.

This book portrays a gifted young man of determination, inspiration and dedication who would not accept the limitations imposed by others in his ambition of becoming an accomplished artist. My desire is for children to gain an understanding of what it takes to achieve their life goals just like Dean Mitchell.

I am pleased that Dean has approved this sketch of his life and has endorsed the use of his paintings to share with readers as well.

Chapter 1
Childhood Days in Quincy

This is the story of Dean Mitchell, a boy who grew up in a small, rural Southern community, his home, not much more than a shack. His mother, Hazel gave him to his grandmother at the age of eleven months; his father was seldom discussed. These were the harsh realities of a boy who earned success as an artist with sheer determination and hard work.

A cool breeze blew through the front door to the other end of the small wooden house as Marie Mitchell, a petite, coffee-colored lady, sat in the worn chair gazing at the eleven-month-old baby who lay in the little white crib. He was her grandson, Dean, the child that she had taken to raise as her own. The bright-eyed baby boy wrapped in a tattered blanket looked up at his grandmother with a strange sense of curiosity as though he understood what was happening. Marie, stern-faced and resolute, was moved by compassion and a sense of duty to this infant who bore her family name. She was determined to raise the boy even though she was already the only caregiver for her ailing mother and it had been many years since she cared for a baby.

Marie was convinced that a college education for her youngest daughter would open career opportunities far beyond those available to her with only a high school degree. So, when Hazel told Marie of her plan to drop out of school and seek local employment, Marie insisted that she reconsider; she desperately wanted one of her four children to get a college education and the career opportunities that a secondary education would afford. Marie offered to raise the boy and her daughter left for college a few days later, leaving the fair-skinned, frail infant in the care of his grandmother. Marie, who Dean would later give the nickname, Grandma, embraced the boy lovingly in her arms in a way that can only be described as a grandmother's hug, knowing the difficulties that were ahead of them; the needs of this innocent child now outweighed all other concerns.

Times were hard for Marie Mitchell and her small family. She worked on the farms during tobacco season, cooked and cleaned for a wealthy family, and later when she could no longer work, received financial assistance from the government. More times than she cared to remember, welfare checks were her only source of income and means of survival. She tried to shield the baby boy from the stigma associated with their poverty and dependence on welfare checks, as it was a reality that she did not want him to know.

Many days and nights Marie Mitchell sat alone in her sparsely furnished house and wondered how she could earn enough money to meet the needs of the family. Her mother needed constant daily attention; the house, though small and always in need of repair, was

another expense; her daughter also needed financial support, as she often ran short of her financial obligations. It was a burden greater than Marie cared to think about as she rubbed her gray hair with her wrinkled and labor-toughened hands.

Through it all, Marie learned to accept the plight that life had given, with a strong conviction that all things would get better somehow. Regardless of their circumstances you could see a smile appear on her face when the bright-eyed youngster toddled into the room. She would always take him in her arms and hold him closely.

"Don't worry son, I'm gone' take care of you, even it takes my last dime," she said. The two shared such a special bond that his grandmother soon became the mother figure in his life, becoming his life raft and a source of inspiration. Hazel visited the boy during summer quarter and Christmas breaks from college.

Dean enjoyed living with his grandmother in the simple-life, small town of Quincy. He felt safe in the Pepper Hill neighborhood where adults looked after all children, regardless of whose family they belonged. When a child was misbehaving, the neighborhood adults would chastise them as they would their own, later reporting such behavior to their parents; this would mean another chastening.

The lad grew so fast that the clothes Marie and Hazel purchased seemed to fit for only a few months and Marie insisted that the boy was always dressed in clean clothes. Dean later learned that his mother often sent clothing and put his needs ahead of her own, probably due to the guilt she felt in leaving the child to continue her education. Marie washed their clothes almost every day in the big wash pot over a fire in the back yard and Dean often helped to hang them on their clothesline to dry in the cool breeze.

Grandmother Marie provided excellent care for the boy she had grown used to calling "her little gift." She often sat quietly in her favorite chair at the small dinner table in the corner of the kitchen and watched him play with wooden blocks and jar lids he often used as toys. When he was old enough to understand, Dean inquired about his mother who visited only during quarter breaks at college. As he matured the visits grew less frequent and Dean had to suppress his feelings of abandonment and appreciate the loving care and adoration of his grandmother, Marie.

Chapter 2
Painting By Numbers

Saturday was one of the highlights of Dean's childhood. He enjoyed his weekly trip to town with his grandmother when she went to shop for groceries. She would often give him five dollars, which was a lot of money for a youth in the 1960's. With money in hand, he ran to the toy aisle while his grandmother shopped for household essentials.

His grandmother and most of her friends shopped or just gathered in the small store to catch up on community news, mostly who had recently died or given birth. This sort of news was important to the few who gathered every Saturday; they were genuinely concerned about their neighbors.

When they returned home, his grandmother always inquired about what Dean had purchased, since she insisted they could not waste money on meaningless frills.

"What did you buy today?" she asked. Dean reached into his bag and proudly pulled out an oil paint-by-number set. He searched her eyes, seeking approval for his selection. Grandma said, "What you gone do with that?" Dean smiled and said, "I am going to paint you a picture."

With great eagerness and anticipation he rushed into his room and closed the door. Dean opened the treasured purchase and slowly sat on the bed in his cozy

little room. The set contained several bottles of colored paints and printed sheets with black and white illustrations, containing tiny numbers at precise locations. Each number indicated a specific color of paint to be applied onto the allotted spaces in each illustration. He carefully dipped the little brush into the paint and began to fill in the areas. His excitement and anticipation were hard to describe as he began, with tempered fear, hoping not to make a mistake on his first artistic creation. Satisfaction soon filled his heart as the mundane black and white illustration came to life with brilliant colors, each component of the painting displaying a character of its own.

Dean emerged from the room after what seemed like hours with a smile on his face and proudly presented the painting to his grandmother.

"That's good Baby," Grandma said. She smiled with a sense of pride and continued washing the dishes in the dimly illuminated kitchen where they spent many hours at the family dinner table. Grandma cherished each of these occasions when Dean shared his artistic creations with her. He was the source

of her inspiration, just as she was to him, and now that her mother had passed away, Grandmother Marie devoted more of her time to Dean's daily activities.

Dean's love of painting grew as the years went by. He no longer needed the paint-by-number sets, but created his own works of art and proudly displayed the finished paintings on the walls of his bedroom to share with his family and friends. Most of his childhood friends did not exhibit much appreciation for his paintings since they were more interested in playing ball in the narrow red clay road that ran in front of the row of small neighborhood houses.

At age eight, Dean went to work in the tobacco fields to assist with family expenses. His initial thoughts of working in the giant fields were frightening for Dean, since he had often heard about the backbreaking labor in the tobacco fields and stories of rattle snakes that sometimes lurked in the mile-long tobacco rows. However, he had no alternative at his age and his small earnings helped to supplement the family's income. Almost everyone in his community toiled in the fields from early morning to almost dusk for menial wages. Tobacco was the lifeblood of the small community with businesses and laborers alike depending on that industry as the mainstay of the local economy.

Each morning, the large blue bus came rolling down the red clay road to pick up the neighborhood adults and children who were old enough to work in the tobacco fields. His cousins and most of his friends were among the large group of field hands, so this helped to calm Dean's fears. The old bus transported them several miles in their daily journey to the fields where everyone exited the same stairs and went to work without complaint.

Painting by Dean Mitchell

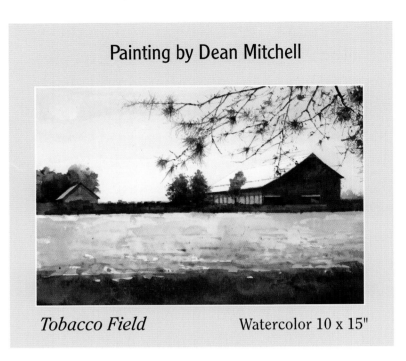

Tobacco Field   Watercolor 10 x 15"

There were multiple rows of tobacco plants topped with heavy, white cloth that had been erected overhead on shade wire, creating a tent-like structure over the plants to keep them partially shaded. Underneath the shade cloth the fragile plants required a lot of care to reach maturity without becoming spotted from overexposure to the Florida sun or eaten by insects.

The shade cloth did little to lessen the summer heat, bearing down on the sweating laborers as they baked in the scorching sun. Dean frowned as he looked up at the giant leaves and tall stalks. But before the day was over, the small-framed boy had learned to lug tobacco and when he was older, he learned how to prime the tobacco like the more mature boys.

When fall came, Dean and other neighborhood children gathered pecans from the pecan trees throughout the community. Dean filled large burlap sacks with the nuts; at the end of each day, they would deliver the nuts to Mr. Earnest's store where he purchased them for cash. Dean was sometimes discouraged by the slow rate that pecans fell of their own accord, so he often climbed the trees to loosen them by shaking the limbs. Though his grandmother would not have approved of such dangerous behavior, he gained the reputation of the best tree climber in the neighborhood; to him this meant more money for his grandmother and him. Occasionally, he bought hamburgers with some of his earnings at the restaurant just down the street when he grew tired of ox tails and rice or neck bones and greens, which his grandmother served regularly. This was a rare treat because his earnings were needed to supplement the family's income.

Painting by Dean Mitchell

Mr. Earnest Pecan Shop   Watercolor 22 x 30"

When he wasn't working, Dean enjoyed spending his early childhood days playing outside in the yard with community friends until the sweltering heat and the seasonal gnats chased them to a shade tree and the faucet in the back yard for a drink of water and time to cool off. Grandmother Marie's love for the boy was evident when she took him to church and showed him off to her friends; her face lit up with pride and adoration every time she spoke of him. Marie taught Dean the meaning of self-reliance and to respect all people, regardless of their race or financial worth.

Dean began discovering more about life while growing up in Quincy, a bedroom community of Florida's capital city, Tallahassee. When Dean was twelve, he accepted an arduous, but better-paying job at the agriculture cannery. Most residents worked the tobacco fields or worked at the agricultural cannery where vegetables were processed and canned for sale later in grocery stores.

In their neighborhood, there were men who gathered at the corner to play cards and indulge in illicit activities; some drank themselves into early graves. Dean's uncle Ben was one of those at the corner and he occasionally asked Dean to go to the nearby store to purchase cigarettes and alcoholic beverages for him. When Marie learned of his outrageous conduct, she scolded both Dean and his uncle in a way they would never forget. After that day, Marie did her best to protect the boy from those she knew could bring him harm or influence him in the wrong direction. She encouraged him to stay away from high school dropouts or those who were involved in illegal activities. His respect for the values and rules of conduct taught by his grandmother gave him the strength to resist

these temptations and stay away from illegal drugs and those who used them.

On days when Marie cleaned the house and washed clothes, she chose the opportunity to instruct Dean in these important skills.

"You need to learn how to take care of yourself son. I'm not going to be around for ever, and you need to know about cooking and cleaning," she said.

After finishing his daily chores, Dean spent a lot of time in his room with the door closed while his grandmother was in the kitchen preparing their meals; painting was now his favorite pastime.

Chapter 3
Moving To Philadelphia

As Dean grew older he became wiser about the world around him and soon realized how poor his family was even though the families of most of his friends were in a similar financial condition. He wanted so much to make life easier for his grandmother, who always taught him to live within his means and to be thankful for what he had. Marie Mitchell was content with her lot in life and taught Dean that they were rich in many ways. In his thoughts, Dean often said, "Some day, I'll be able to buy my grandmother everything her heart desires."

One day, Dean came home to find his grandmother very ill. He worked day and night to care for his grandmother and keep up the household chores. Through his care, she improved and regained much of her strength. However, it soon became apparent that she could not adequately care for the growing youth, so Dean and his grandmother moved to Philadelphia, to live with his aunt. During this time, his mother was able to visit on weekends to help nurse Marie since Hazel had now graduated from college and was employed at a local hospital.

During a weekend visit, his mother became curious as to why Dean spent such long periods of time alone in his bedroom. When she entered his bedroom, she found Dean engrossed in one of his paintings and asked coldly, "Why do you waste so much of your time with that art stuff, boy? You should be studying your books so you can go to college one day, so you can be somebody."

Dean knew she did not understand; he ignored her comments and continued painting.

Dean enjoyed trips to the local newsstands where he spent hours browsing publications such as *Life Magazine* and *The Saturday Evening Post*, which often displayed illustrated covers and text illustrations by famous artists like Norman Rockwell. Upon returning home, he pulled out his paper, pencils, markers, and watercolor paints and tried to recreate their illustrations from memory. He stared intently at each of his imitations, dreaming of becoming a famous artist, his creations inspiring the whole world.

One day while flipping through old magazines his aunt often kept on the coffee table Dean noticed an advertisement for a correspondence course from a famous art school. Overcome with excitement, he completed the application, sealed it carefully, and placed it in the mail.

A few weeks later, a well-dressed stranger appeared at the door of his aunt's home. His mother was in Philadelphia on a visit that day; she answered the door, greeting a man who said he represented the art school. Dean stood quietly in an adjacent room eavesdropping with a bashful expression on his face, for he had not previously discussed his intentions with his family.

When the man told his mother the cost of the course from such a prestigious school, she immediately said no, due to their precarious financial state.

After his mother closed the door behind the representative, she immediately called Dean into the room and scolded him harshly for sending the application in the mail. "You don't know enough about art to become a real artist," she said. "And besides, who will buy it? You are just going to end up on the streets trying to become an artist. You need to spend

your time learning something you can earn a living from, and art is not it."

Tears welled up in the eyes of the young boy; he retreated quietly to his tiny room and lay face down on the bed. Dean sobbed for hours that day and again each time he thought about his mother's words for several days. Slowly the dream of a diploma from the prestigious art school faded, but his fascination with art became stronger with each new painting he completed. It seemed to Dean that his family continually tried to discourage his dreams of a career in art due to financial considerations. His mother even told him that few people of his color were known to buy art and her statement was accurate during this period of U.S. history.

"Only rich people buy art," she told him. She could not envision any of them buying art painted by a boy from the South who was black.

Since his aunt tightly controlled his allowance, he began secretly saving his lunch money to purchase art supplies and continued painting, drawing and creating, as he spent even more time alone in his room. Dean ignored the family's discouraging remarks, because he understood that his mother was trying to protect him from hurt and the disappointment of a failed career choice.

After three years in Philadelphia, Dean received news that brightened his day. He and his grandmother were going back to Quincy, the place he had always called home. He looked forward to seeing his old friends again. Though he was now a teenager in the ninth grade, he retained the same innocent and shy disposition as when he left for Philadelphia. Yet, his love for painting had grown even deeper.

Painting by Dean Mitchell

Back Road to Quincy   Watercolor 7.5 x 10"

Chapter 4
High School Days

Now in high school, Dean signed up for art class. Though he was a good student, none of the other classes mattered as much to Dean. His art instructor that year, Tom Harris, taught him a lot about drawing and painting techniques with oils and watercolor. Harris took special interest in each of the students and their artistic abilities. He provided transportation to art fairs and encouraged them to enter their paintings in various art exhibitions throughout the region.

Each boy in his class was artistically talented. In Dean's mind, his work did not measure up to that of some of the other students and he became discouraged. His extended family did not do much to encourage him during this time as they often teased him by calling attention to the awards earned by the other boys.

Finally his hard work and determination paid

off. One of his paintings won first place in an
art competition. He could hardly wait to share
the good news with his grandmother. When he
entered the door of his home, his grandmother knew from his wide smile that he had accomplished something special. He held up the
awards, excitedly swinging them back and forth
in the air with pride.

"I won, Grandma," the excited young man
said, peering up at his grandmother. His grandmother sat down to get a thorough look at the
awards in his hands.

"That's good honey, I'm so proud of you," she
said.

Dean's face lit up even brighter. There would

be many similar occasions when Dean returned home after submitting his paintings in art competitions. Each time, his grandmother prepared his favorite meal featuring her special fried chicken and the two sat down to discuss each trip with Mr. Harris and his classmates.

These experiences increased his conviction to pursue a career in art despite his family's sentiments. Mr. Harris had opened Dean's eyes to a larger world of art, convincing him that he had a special talent and that he must find a way to attend art school to enhance his ability.

Dean later attended Shanks High School where he met Mr. Hudson, his new art teacher who recognized his talent and dedication. By now, Dean had earned a reputation in high school for his

artistic talents and this bolstered his confidence and determination to pursue more training. His paint-by-number days were far behind him now; his beautiful original art was a testament to his ever-increasing confidence and talent.

Each year, along with the essentials of math, science, and social studies, an art course was included on his class schedule. Dean always received an "A⁺" from his art teachers.

Dean was proud to be part of an accomplished group of artists in high school. They felt a great sense of satisfaction and pride when the students and teachers noticed their artwork at the school.

When high school graduation day came, Dean beamed with pride and fulfillment; most of his schoolmates knew that he had been accepted at The Columbus School of Art and Design in Columbus, Ohio. He was uncertain and a little fearful of leaving home, especially about leaving his aged grandmother, yet both of them knew that he should go. He mused about the times he had spent alone in his room painting: "I guess I'll miss those times."

In his heart, there was a part of Dean that wanted to stay where he felt safe, but he knew he must follow his dreams since he was determined to pursue a career in art. By now his family knew that he was serious about becoming a career artist. Though his mother and aunt accepted his choice, they both felt they should issue one last stern warning that in pursuing his dream, he would probably become a beggar living on the streets. Dean ignored their warnings and prepared to leave for college, determined to pursue a career in art.

Chapter 5
Off to College

College life and being out on his own posed a host of new obstacles and responsibilities for Dean but the values instilled by his grandmother always brought him through. Through the years, Dean grew more accustomed to living away from home and became consumed with his love of painting. At The Columbus School of Art and Design, his skills really improved, but he soon learned that the prestigious school was nothing like high school, nor were the teachers at all like Mr. Harris.

Dean also struggled in his own mind to compete with other students, many from affluent families who had the financial means to travel to art galleries and to provide the advantage of art tutors. He felt that his paintings were in some ways inferior; this was hard for him to accept. Sometimes in moments of despair, feelings of self-doubt filled his eyes with tears. On more than one occasion when his frustrations became overwhelming, he thought about giving up and returning home to his old job at the cannery.

"What would Grandma think of me?" he mused. "I don't want to disappoint her."

Grandma's familiar words haunted him: "You can do anything you set your mind to if you work hard enough," she often repeated to encourage him. Then, he reminded himself, "If it is going to be, it is up to me."

These words gave him comfort and the strength to rise above the temptation to return to his old job at the cannery, since he knew that would be taking the easy way out of an adversity. He remembered the harsh words of his mother, and so many others who did not believe that he could be successful as an artist when he was a young boy. These words made him angry and even more determined to succeed, proving to everyone and even to himself that he had indeed chosen the right path. From that day on he made up in his mind that he would work hard and succeed, no matter the personal sacrifice.

"I will not end up on the streets, and I will become an artist," Dean said, resolving to study even harder.

He searched the library for books on watercolor techniques by various artists, which he studied constantly.

Soon Dean's work began to improve and he now gripped his brush with a renewed sense of confidence. The watercolor and oil paintings became his friends and now Dean knew that a life on the streets or back at the cannery would not be his destiny. Occasionally, Dean did return to work in the Quincy cannery, but only briefly during the summers to earn sufficient money to continue his education.

While home on summer breaks, he grew more observant of the lifestyle of the people of Quincy. He now studied the detail of the local buildings, old tobacco barns and schools with a wonderfully new perspective.

"This is who I am," Dean thought to himself.

"There's no denying it."

Dean found that images he wanted to illustrate were related to his childhood: old tobacco barns and churches, the detailed depiction of African Americans in their daily lives, the pictures of rustic buildings, and the people of his time, all captured the true essence of his childhood.

After each summer was over, Dean was sad about leaving his Grandmother Marie but eager to return to school and continue training. By now he was close to graduating and this brought great excitement and anticipation to the boy who had come so far. His hobby of art had developed into a profession and many of the paintings now captured a touch of history as he experienced it. His memories of Quincy, his childhood acquaintances, Sundays in church and those of his grandmother provided an abundance of images to illustrate, for his memory kept a vivid picture of daily existence in the small Southern town. He realized that the images of his past were the things that made him the person he was now becoming. He began to develop a renewed sense of appreciation for the people and events that had helped to shape him.

Dean continued entering his paintings in contests where he won many awards. He once entered an art exhibition in Panama City, Florida and was awarded two U. S. Saving Bonds for his work. Small gallery owners throughout Florida began to take note of Dean's art and his work began to command top prices, even while he was still in college. The people were impressed with his artistic abilities as well as the humility and genuineness of the young man.

While there, he was introduced to a person who offered him a job teaching in the Boys and Girls Club, making ten dollars an hour. Many boys in the organization were from similar environments as Dean, so he was especially happy to share his artistic talents with them.

As time went by, art school became even more enjoyable to Dean. He became closely acquainted with some of his fellow art students and learned something from each of them. He also learned that art is universal; it is presented in many colors, yet sees neither color nor race. With that understanding, Dean graduated from art school.

Chapter 6
An Artist Evolves

Graduation day was the most joyous day of his life. His family came to celebrate his success; on that day, even his mother was smiling.

"What am I to do now?" Dean asked himself, standing alone in his small apartment.

"I am not making enough money selling art, and I don't have a job to take care of myself. I don't want to go back home to Quincy, now that I have a college degree. Besides, Quincy is not the ideal place for selling art."

Frustration and discouragement again entered the young man's thoughts so he telephoned his grandmother and confided his concerns. Of course, his grandmother wanted him

to be near her, and she lacked any experience in the world of art, so she persuaded him to come back and work at the cannery for the immediate future until he found a job more suited for his talent and training.

Dean was disappointed, but knew from experience that his grandmother's advice was usually sound, so he returned to Quincy to work again at his old job in the cannery.

After a few weeks Dean received a telephone call. A friendly voice on the other end of the line extended an invitation for him to come to Kansas City for a job interview with Hallmark, the internationally famous greeting card company. He could hardly catch his breath as the excitement was more than he could handle. He had never been to Kansas City, but was elated to hear of the prospect of employment in the field of his artistic training with such a prestigious company.

Dean packed a few items and boarded the bus for Kansas City. The bus trip took all day, but knowing what the ride could mean filled every mile with anticipation.

When the interview was completed, Dean was offered the job with a starting salary greater than he had ever earned.

He thought, "Imagine, Dean Mitchell, a native of the small town of Quincy, Florida has now earned a college degree in art and just landed a job with an internationally famous company."

"Kansas City, here I come!"

The next few weeks were spent packing the watercolor paintings on which he was presently working along with his few personal belongings and moved into a small, but conveniently located apartment in a suburb of Kansas City. Dean adjusted easily to his new home and loved working at Hallmark where he quickly developed a kindred relationship with his fellow employees, some of whom reminded him of friends from home. Again, Dean spent most of his free time at his small, yet quaint apartment painting and he continued to enter his paintings in contests and art shows, both nationally and internationally.

After a few months, it became apparent to Dean that his current employment would not afford the latitude to exercise his talents in the way he desired. Dean wanted his boss to understand the kind of art he wanted to depict on greeting cards, but he felt that the time was not yet right for that discussion. He wanted to prove himself to his new boss and then present some of his own ideas. However, in spite of his attempts to adhere to his boss' instructions, his frustration soon led to dissention between them, the pressure of which really affected his output at work. The resulting distraction became apparent to his boss and after several encounters his boss called him into his office and fired him. Dean was devastated. What was he going to do? How was he going to pay his bills and other responsibilities? The pressure and loss of income brought an end to this part of his career that he worked so hard to achieve.

Dean remembered the chilling remarks his mother had made throughout his childhood and after high school graduation, and the thought of being homeless really made him fearful. Tears filled his eyes as he sat in the small self-designed studio in his apartment wondering what he was going to do. His mind focused on the words of his grandmother, Marie. She had strong moral fiber and had always wanted the best for the child she had raised from the age of eleven months. She understood him and always believed in him. He took his grandmother's picture from the nightstand and hugged it closely in his arms.

"I will make it as an artist, you'll see," he said sobbingly.

"I will not disappoint you, Grandma. I may not have riches but I have my dignity, and that is more important."

He had survived the harsh realities of an impoverished childhood even with the absence of his parents. He had also toiled in the long rows of tobacco for years, so this setback was just one more obstacle he must find a way to overcome. This may have been the end of his job with Hallmark, but his life was far from over. In fact, it was just beginning and this apparent setback would prove to be the beginning of his career as a full-time artist.

Dean continued to enter his paintings in national and international competitions, which now seemed to be his only hope for survival. He was not happy about disappointing his supervisor at Hallmark, or his inability to convince him of the merit of his artistic concepts. Now, he had to put his troubles behind him and focus on his dream of becoming a famous artist.

From 1988 to 1999 he had won 74 awards, and over time, his resume' amassed over 400 awards. Among his honors is the grand prize of $50,000 from the Arts of the Parks in 1991.

The first competition he entered in Kansas City won two awards. Surprised and elated, Dean rushed to telephone his grandmother. He had competed with many great artists, and he had won!

"I'm so proud of you!" grandma said. "I knew you wuz aimin' for somethin' good."

In a few years, Dean had won more than two hundred major awards, including first prize at London England's T.H. Saunders International Artist and Watercolor Show, the National Watercolor Society, the Art of the Parks Medal for Overall Excellence and Hubbard Art Award for Excellence.

Soon the name of Dean Mitchell was recognized throughout the art world. He had proven to everyone that by applying attributes of determination, dedication and hard work, you can achieve anything you desire. The more art competitions he entered, the more awards and recognition he gained.

"This is good," he thought. "But I can do better."

Chapter 7
Painting About Life

Dean learned that creating quality art was hard work, but he was determined to make this his career. In his small apartment studio, he made painting his life, often reminding himself, "If it's going to be, it's up to me." He spent days, evenings and many nights creating watercolors and oil paintings that portrayed the tales he remembered from childhood, bringing times and places of the past to life on canvas.

The finished paintings always made him smile as he pondered the stories that lived deep within each created image. It was a good feeling, one that he wanted to continue experiencing over and over again with each new work of art.

On a spring day some years later, while working on an unfinished project, Dean received a phone call from a renowned art gallery, inviting him to feature some of his best work in an upcoming art exhibition. While Dean was overjoyed, the old feelings of fear and doubt appeared in his mind.

"Who would have thought that I would be featured in a famous art gallery," Dean asked himself with "goose bumps" covering his small framed body.

Will they like my work? Will they want to buy what I have created? Will they understand the messages I am trying to convey? What if no one comes?"

While the questions and uncertainties continued, these did not stop him from preparing for the big show.

"This could be my big chance," he thought.

Soon his doubts and fears were put to rest as friends, relatives and many strangers came, purchasing Dean's paintings for top-dollar prices. As the guests asked questions about his work, he was pleased with the spectrum of reactions. There were smiles, frowns, and gasps of silent awe while others just stared in speechless admiration. They were expressing just the reactions he had always dreamed of.

"They get it, they understand what my

paintings are conveying," Dean said to himself. This moment was the confirmation and source of inspiration he needed, for he now knew what he would be doing with his life.

For a brief moment, Dean drifted again back to memories of when he first began painting with the paint-by-number set. He thought of Grandma and smiled, remembering her sense of satisfaction and approval while she urged him to follow his dreams and to always do his best. He felt this was the beginning of something great!

A few years later, Dean received yet another phone call from the Quincy Art Center; the director at the newly opened gallery asked him to be the *featured artist* at an art show to raise funds for the center. Finally, Dean was going back home to share his accomplishments and his paintings with the people who unknowingly had inspired his work with a heart and soul. He began sifting through the beautiful watercolor and oil paintings he had spent so many hours creating, choosing one painting after another to display at his show. One painting brought a big wide smile to his face, as it had always been one of his favorites; the

Painting by Dean Mitchell

Grandmother   Acrylic 9.25 x 14.25"

first portrait of his grandmother. He had given special attention to creating the image that expressed his feelings for the woman he admired and adored so much and was the source of such inspiration for his life.

Dean wondered if the small town of his childhood was ready for what he now had to offer. He wanted the people who were the subjects of the stories chronicled through his paintings to come to his show, and many of them did. Along with Grandma, his friends

and relatives stood by his side. Dean felt
so proud. It was like a family reunion. He
recognized some of his teachers and classmates, though he had not seen most of them
for many years. The event was a greater success than he could have imagined.

Dean still enjoys his brief visits back home,
each one providing him with a sense of clar-
ity and meaning far beyond the beautifully
colored images of his paintings. His dream of

becoming a famous artist had now, indeed, come true. Dean's oil and watercolor paintings are now featured in art galleries throughout the United States.

Today, he is a nationally recognized artist with dozens of awards attesting to his ability. His work can be found in the permanent collections of the St. Louis Art Museum, Nelson-Atkins Museum of Art and Kemper Museum of Contemporary Arts of Kansas City, Missouri, the Nerman Museum of Contemporary Art in Overland Park, Kansas and many more. He also designed a U.S. postage stamp.

Dean now wears a salt-and-pepper

53

beard but the boyish appearance that always brought a smile to his grandmother's face is still there. Marie Mitchell, his favorite fan, continued to live in Quincy for many years after Dean became famous. His return to the small town always caused the residents to take note. He continues to be invited back to receive awards and share his artwork, many of which are now worth thousands of dollars. Dean spends most of his time painting and traveling to art exhibitions. His dream for the future is to use art to instruct children all over the world; to have them look at his paintings and say, "Hey, I can do that too."

Dean has always wanted to increase children's appreciation of art and to change the stereotypical perception of the South through his paintings. So he painted scenes of the neighborhood in which he grew up, with the hope that people would embrace the stories of hope, love, sorrow, struggle, peace, faith, and joy depicted with his brush.

Additionally, he wants people to see the positive side of Black America in the stories of his upbringing depicted through his art.

"African American children still do not envision themselves becoming successful artists," he says. "In order for this attitude to change, schools need to spend more time teaching about African American artists, so that children can see black people painting themselves and think, someone like me painted that.

Painting by Dean Mitchell

Leading the Young   Oil Painting 18 x 24"

These will be artists that they can identify more closely with than a Rembrandt or a Picasso; artists not only of a different time, but a different complexion and culture as well."

Dean takes every opportunity to instruct children of the dedication it took for him to fulfill his goal in becoming a self-supporting artist and to encourage them in considering art as a career.

"It is like seeing Tiger Woods playing golf," Dean says. " The more African American children see black artists, the sooner their underlying image will change. My work is not about color; it is about life. The more they see the images of successful artists, the more they can envision themselves becoming artists."

Dean enjoys painting about simple yet pro-found epics passed down through Southern history. Raised by his grandmother in a small, quaint Florida town, his creative imagery portrays story elements that evolved from childhood life experiences. In a series of paint-ings Dean portrays his hometown of Quincy, Florida, the first titled, "Quincy's Boarding House." Teachers often rented rooms there when they first moved to Quincy, soldiers and other out-of-towners spent weekends at the boarding house and it was the permanent residence for others. The large two-story house was popular for many years, but the building became vacant and in disrepair. Bushes and weeds now cover the corner lot where the old, abandoned boarding house sits. The rusted tin roof, the broken boards and windows of the house that Dean realistically painted allows the viewer to recapture the past, gain some understanding of the present, and imagine the future. Though the future of the old boarding house is uncertain, Dean's painting gives life to a time that is no more.

Old tobacco barns enliven some of Dean's art, the images portraying the days when he worked Quincy's tobacco fields. He paints pictures of the times when "tobacco was king." The industry was the main source of income for many Gadsden County residents where tobacco-growing landowners became wealthy supplying the quality outside wrapping for cigars. The work was arduous in the sweltering heat of the tobacco fields. Dean and his schoolmates met and played in the fields; now he captures these vignettes with his brush and canvas.

Painting by Dean Mitchell

Tobacco Barn   Watercolor 20 x 15"

Likewise, Dean has recently painted a series of images of the French Quarter in New Orleans. His images of dilapidated houses and historic buildings reveal the moods, attitudes and details of the people who lived there. One watercolor is entitled "Sunny Day in the Quarter," a simplistic painting of a man with an umbrella on a horse-drawn buggy in front of a picturesque New Orleans building. He creates images that cause people to reminisce about the city's vast history. The New Orleans series of 150 paintings, will be displayed in a soon-to-be-released book.

Painting by Dean Mitchell

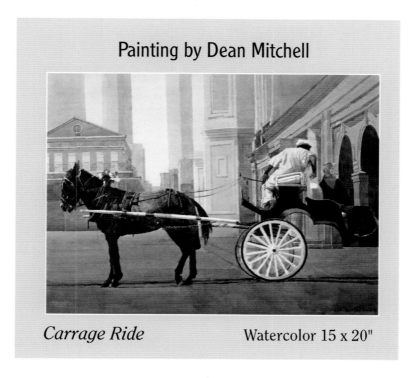

Carrage Ride   Watercolor 15 x 20"

Painting by Dean Mitchell

DEAN MITCHELL AWS ©07

French Quarter Alley   Watercolor 15 x 10"

Another series very special to Dean is that of his family, the one of his Grandmother, Marie being his favorite. She was an enduring influence on his life and art. Her teaching and ideals are the strong thread that is intertwined through his art and his love and respect for her is clearly evident. She believed in him when no one else did and taught him moral values and to respect all people. His love and respect for his grandmother is the reason he now enjoys depicting other elderly people.

Dean's paintings allow the viewer to encounter people, places and events of times past. Art lovers often stand, staring for a long time in silence, then smile, and finally move on to another painting, only to repeat the same reaction. The time spent in a small Florida town helped to shape his paintings. He, like most artists, paints what he knows. His dream to travel this path was conceived early in his life and supported and encouraged by a grandmother who believed in him and taught him to never give up.

An art club for children in Quincy was established in Dean Mitchell's name to help children discover their artistic talents.

"It takes dedication, determination, and hard work to become a great artist," Dean said.

"Great artists paint pictures and create stories for others to read and they leave it up to the viewer to decide how the art relates to their life experiences. It is up to the artist to create pictures that continue to tell stories while the meaning and level of emotion each contain are different for everyone."

Is he famous? That depends on your perception. Dean Mitchell considers himself as just an ordinary person from a small town in the Florida Panhandle who began to discover his artistic ability as a youth.

"I knew I wanted

to be an artist, but I did not know then that I would one day sell my artwork for money," Dean often says.

"Art is something I really enjoy. It is not only my hobby, but my dream that later became my lifelong vocation."

Dean Mitchell

Priceless Treasures   Watercolor 24 x 18"